Girl by the Water

Girl by the Water

by Gary Geddes

Turnstone Press

Turnstone Press
607-100 Arthur Street
Winnipeg, Manitoba
Canada R3B 1H3

Turnstone Press gratefully acknowledges the assistance of the Canada Council and the Manitoba Arts Council.

Cover art: *Camouflage* © 1974 David Mayrs

Text design: Gary Geddes

This book was printed and bound in Canada by Kromar Printing for Turnstone Press.

Canadian Cataloguing in Publication Data
Geddes, Gary, 1940-
Girl by the water
Poems.
ISBN 0-88801-178-4
I. Title.
PS8563.E3G4 1994 C811'.54 C93-098203-7
PR9199.3.G43G4 1994

The author would like to thank the following publications, where some of these poems have appeared, or will appear: *Globe & Mail, The Review, The Canadian Forum, Ontario Federation of Agriculture Newsletter, The Capilano Review, Quarry, Orbis, Literary Olympians, 1992: An International Anthology, This Magazine, Poetry Canada Review*, and *Border Crossings.*

Table of Contents

III. Two Moose on the Hunker Creek Road

IV. Relative Humidity

V. Mao, Dreaming

It takes so little, so infinitely little, for a person to cross the border beyond which everything loses meaning: love, conviction, faith, history. Human life—and herein lies its secret—takes place in the immediate proximity of that border, even in direct contact with it; it is not miles away, but a fraction of an inch.

Milan Kundera

I. Girl by the Water

Artist

Only the girl by the water attracts me.
Soldiers, with pomp and pretension, parading colours
in the distant square, mean nothing.

Hair ochre, not auburn; head tilted a little forward, nape
bare to wind or axe or lover's mouth.
The quiet ache her beauty causes reverberates
back along the taut thread of my being to its obscure
and infinitessimal beginnings.

Yes, yes, you say, fanciful talk,
a doddering antiquity
passing off each urge (or demi-urge) as aesthetics;
skip the rhetoric, give us the old
blind thrust in the dark.
Humour the artist; you'll not find
Eros lacking in the oils.

She peers intently at something in her palm, perhaps
a map of the future. Will there be children?
Will one come to grief, and how
to endure that? Amused
by reminders, in a congruence of lines,
but not foolish enough
to think these qualities a guarantee.

Without lowering her hand, she looks
across the water and locates
the wavering V of departing geese. Though young,
she is no stranger to loss. Sounds

these travellers make recall her to a simple errand
not yet completed. She gathers her skirts
and begins to run towards the square, the milling soldiers,
where, lamb to slaughterer's blade, she surrenders
her heart for the hint of a smile.

Chamber Maid

She had clogs in one hand, money in the other.
I was there on the pier, close enough
to see her count the coins
and drop them into an apron pocket.

We worked together mornings
at the inn, five 'til noon.
A dozen reeking chamber pots,
wood, ironing, beds to make;
it took us hours to scrub the smell of piss
and ashes from our hands.

The man in question was not old.
Whatever business brought him into town
would not detain him long.
I'd guess the coach was hired;
the horses, though freshly groomed,
were unnaturally lean
and one, a gelding, would not stop
chewing on the bit.

I thought she shuddered
once or twice
before she turned to leave.
I'm still amazed to think
her feet were bare.

Priest

She had something to confess.
I was half asleep
and did not catch the details.

To tell the truth, I was having trouble
concentrating on the petty sins
of parishioners, when I had my own lusts
to contend with. Gluttony, choir-boys,
Christ's blood by the gallon.

She spoke of voices.
This was new in one so young.

Her breasts were exquisitely formed,
though tightly bound;
and I could faintly distinguish
something on her wrist
when she made the sign of the cross.
It might have been a birth-mark
or a bruise. *Mea culpa.*

I erred, so be it;
I didn't want to miss the arrival
of the boats with their catch
of fresh cod. A thousand
Hail Marys every four hours,
before meals. Later,
when I saw her at the shore

listening to her voices,
I couldn't shake
this tag of schoolboy Latin:

Menses, menses,
the Lord's amanuensis.

Aunt

Who could blame her for those hours by the river,
where it bellies out and wind catches the sails
of sea-going vessels. She was wearing the vest
with the velvet smocking usually reserved for Sundays,
which I'd given her after my fourth child.
God knows, it would never fit me
again. She spent an afternoon in the window seat
making alterations, cocooned in her thoughts
and a low, tuneless humming. Outside, cobbles
glistened and gave off steam after the sudden
shower; I looked up from my bowl of batter
in time to see two horses rear in their traces
and the coach clatter to an agitated stop. I screamed
and ran to the door to look for my youngest,
leaving doughy prints on the wood and handle.
He'd heard nothing and remained transfixed
by his make-believe saucepan boat and the puddle
that contained it. She stood in the doorway
as the coach rounded the corner, the velvet smocking
aglow in gathered light, and looked at the bright
bead of blood on her thumb. *You frightened me,*
she said, wiping the injured area clean on her tongue.
She seemed so young, I forgave her
the trust she still harboured, the hope,
and for artlessly animating my loutish husband.

Private

They questioned me, of course. Soldiers
are fair game: bastions of good deeds
in battle, but animals in town.
The spoils of war. My own sister
raped, but not by soldiers.

I saw her crouched in an empty stall
in the barn, watching the blood and sperm
drip between her fingers. Years later,
I helped my father die slowly.

My wagon pinned him to the wall
of the granary, while the team
of Belgians, deaf to his cries, danced
on the spot. I was drunk

when the girl entered a shop
and the curtains were drawn; for all I knew,
she was the owner's daughter.

Merchant

A few pennies, no more. There was great noise
and brouhaha in the square, enough
to interfere with my accounts.
A wave of sound swept inside
when the door opened. Otherwise, I might
not have noticed her, bent
over goods and produce at the counter.

Three soldiers lounged in the doorway, tongues
hanging out, and I had to draw the latch
to get rid of them. News of defeat carries fast
and this rough lot was next in line, vessels loading
all day at anchor, coal barges and small skiffs
strung out beside them in the slow current.
Think about it. A pity to go to your grave
ignorant of the other great mystery.
Still, I have no proof.

She toyed with a pear and an apple, then held
a remnant of white muslin to her cheek.
It didn't add up, the vacant look,
the way her fingers brushed the tops
of sundry items. She might have propositioned me
or purchased candies. Instead,
she placed her sweating pennies in the charity box
for the families of lost mariners.
Laughter and shouting, the door closed,
and a small quantity of sand
on the floor.

Lawyer

The only evidence we have that's overriding
is the fact she's disappeared. Guardians
asked us not to publish;
the governing council cautioned,
for the public good, to await news
from the front. My obligation's

to the law. I reconstruct the morning
from myriad clues, then retire
to my club to rinse the foul taste
from my mouth. At night I dream
my own complicity, the violence,
lies, the hot desire. The girl
I search for is six months younger
than the child who eats
at this table, calls me father.

How can I know what she thinks
of me any more than I know the limits
of my own depravity? The hand
she extends, will I cut it off at the wrist
and enter it as evidence?

What kind of advocate is this
who listens to the requiem of pain
and feels his own sex rise.

Midshipman

She had a small anchor,
not much larger than a wasp,
tattooed on her wrist before I left
on the first troopship.

I was in the crow's nest
with a bosun's pipe
when we hoisted the aftersheets.
I could see her on the rocks
of the Eggerton Head promontory
waving, holding up her anchor,
and listening for the three short blasts
I'd promised to make.

I suppose we were lovers,
though without the usual
haste and burning;
I'd touched her naked breasts
and she was not ashamed
to admit her curiosity.
We talked, collected shells
at Eggerton Head, and thought
an earlobe worth an afternoon.

Drowning wasn't half so bad
and I carried that tiny anchor
with me to my grave.

Mother

Who are the real freaks
at the carnival?

Fathers, uncles, educators,
all obsessed with my hole,
prodding me with words, objects,
themselves. Step this way, gentlemen,
see the vortex, the grave,
the black rent
from which all things come
and into which it all disappears.

That's it, pretend you're shocked.

You couldn't even wait for breasts
to advertize my plum, my garden
plot, my anchorage, third
eye you must all investigate,
porthole into paradise
or hell. What could I say to her
as a mother that would be useful
without breaking her heart

or her will? I kept my distance
and my counsel, gave her up
for adoption, and used my earnings
to protect her. She never saw
through my disguise, the rented coach,
the childless couple with their books
and picnic baskets.

Herself

A strong easterly was blowing
off Eggerton Head, so surface driftwood
seemed stationary, despite the fast
current in the narrows. I folded
my clothes neatly in a crevice
above the high-water line and wrapped myself
loosely in white muslin, cutting armholes,
and drawing in the waist with pins
and ribbon. I'd let the merchant cheat me
in my purchases, knowing he was old enough
to be distracted by his greed.

My mother and her favourite customer
would not consent to leave me here
until I confided I'd meet my beau
within the hour. I never loved her more
than at that moment, for her madness
and extravagance. Voices told me
he was dead a week before the news
arrived in town. I made my peace
with God, blessed the aunt who taught me
how to sew, and kissed a drunken soldier
on the cheek before I quit the square.

The wind eased. I formed a whistle
with a blade of grass between my thumbs
and blew three times. Does every bride
have goosebumps? Driftwood moved
towards the sea; the water took me
in its strong embrace.

II. Junkfood Pastoral

Subsidies

A boy with a mechanical arm
addresses a group of kids
on farm safety;
a farmer tries to talk
to the camera—still asking himself
how it happened—youngest son, beside him
one moment on the fender,
slipping under the rear wheel of the tractor.

Eighty percent of rural deaths,
the voice explains,
are the result of farm accidents.

Statistics are no consolation
when you've seen the support-block
give way and the circular saw
walk through the flesh of your son's neck.
At night as you drift towards sleep
you see the recognition
in his startled eyes;
cock's crow
is the engine's whine.

A year later, you still can't look at her
over breakfast, rise
to the need in her flesh
or yours. You toy with an egg,
hard-boiled and intransigent
on your plate, invite
the coffee to burn your lips.

You hear them debate subsidies
in parliament, the future of the family farm,
and you know that nothing you plant
will ever again grow straight,
nothing you do
will ever make it right.

Baltics Corners

It wasn't McCrae, oiled and immobile,
plumbing his emptiness
by the chequered tablecloth,
life a brief buzz of static before
the screen goes blank.

He'd tired of imagining the goings-on
in the converted cheese factory
foreigners had once bulit
at the corner
or wondering why the single mother
across the road
barricaded her yard with sheets
of corrugated metal.

Inhabitants of the nearest village
were no better than the trash
they collected; and those down the road,
perverts and child molesters
(what could you expect
from the French, all that superstition
and idolatry and unable to speak
the language properly),
city people, paying too much for land
and ruining things for the rest
of us with their computers
and fancy ideas.

No, it wasn't McCrae;
it was the cows,
thirty milkers, full to bursting,

abandoned, as if driven
over a buffalo jump, soon too weak to bellow, then
down on their knees from thirst,
hides strung like awnings
over wire frames, bags slack as scrota,
the lucky ones asphyxiated
when they fell twisted
straining against their metal collars.

Rats, first to catch the scent, grew attentive;
then the neighbours, the herd ripe as camembert.
Silly bugger's thrown away his quota,
McLeod said over supper, police gone,
and that fool from the SPCA
with his notebook and tape-recorder,
animals buried, lime an inch deep on the barn floor.

There's no quota on nut-cases around here,
his teenager replied, wiping
the milk-white moustache
from her upper lip.

Junk Food Pastoral

Yours is the worst hay I cut,
Frank tells me, as he hoists another bale
onto the loaded wagon, where his wife
places it in interlocking fashion
over the previous layer, and the boy,
a late and unexpected child,
runs up and down the angled stooks.

I don't see Frank all winter, except to wave
as he drives home to family
and chores from the factory in Ottawa.
He speaks wistfully of retirement,
wondering how much steam he'll still have
when the nine-year-old leaves home.

A low yield this year, nine hundred bales,
fields over-run with straw weed,
hay I first charged him for, then shared,
and am now pleased just to have cut
to keep the thistles and burdock in check.

As the haywagon fills, he uses
the front-end loader with a sheet of plywood
to hoist six bales at a time.
This is their holiday, racing the weather,
ten loads in the heat of the day,
binder-twine burning capable hands.

Rhythm of work. Smiles that take root
in stomach wall or rib-cage—they don't fade easily.

The worst hay, Frank is standing
eight feet above me on his plywood stage,
scenery of fast-moving cloud,
but my cows seem to like it best.

Daylight

How many days of waiting for white stress lines
along the haunches, winking vulva,
tendons strained across the belly.

I get the kids out of bed, more for company
than education, and take them to the barn,
jackets over their nightshirts, where they mount
sawhorses to see into the stall.

Eyes wild, hooves pawing the cement floor
of the stable, then the mare
is down, her hind quarters too close to the wall
and the vet, nonchalant from his party,
telling me over the phone not to fret.

I place the afterbirth, still attached,
over her rump as the manual suggests
and watch, nervously, as she licks
the foal clean, the skewed white marking on its nose
turned towards me in the half-light.

What'll we call him, Dad?

During this time I've forgotten the kids, all
eyes, bare legs shaky as the colt's. Bronwen, the stickler
for details, reminded me earlier to set the clocks
ahead an hour. I forgot. My watch
says 1:00 a.m., but it's later than that,
the whole birth taking as long as the light we save.

Daylight, I say. *We'll call him Daylight.*

Weeping Tiles

The truck from the Moose Creek Septic Company
backs up under the maples and drops
its suctioning hose into the tank of brown sludge
recently unearthed. Fifteen years of domestic soup
percolating, all winter, below the frost line,
the incremental solids gathering volume
while the liquids disperse themselves
along a network of arteries under the lawn,
a cocktail for the fine hairs that line
the fingers of foraging root.

The driver, enormous hoe in hand, stirs
the broth, untroubled by the ripe legend
colouring the afternoon; he squats and balances
on the concrete lip of the sarcophagus
with the expectant air of a fisherman, or the boy
whose straw will soon vanquish a milkshake.
No rich archive to discover,
no reservoir of dreams or deep images—
sediment not sentiment, an antiquated holding-tank
and a violated bed of weeping tiles.

Words like sheep break through the fence
their ears and long black faces
curiously cocked

Sky opaque over Paul's meadow, ragged
where it meets poplars, the dead elm
we agreed to cut down
still standing along the disputed property-line.

Jan could barely make out his words over the roar
of the tractor, as it idled in mid-furrow,
something about Rock Hudson having AIDS.
Paul leaned towards the road, the grin
on his sunburnt face still betraying
the boy who grew up during the war
in Germany and never quite understood
what happened inside him
or the departure of wife and children
here in the new land.
When lightning struck his barn,
leaving only charred remains,
he brought over fuzzy polaroid shots
to prove the fire started from faulty hydro installation,
saying to Jan squinting at the kitchen table,
Do you need glasses, or what?

I never learned
to engage this gruff man,
illiterate and print-shy, yet considered
the best shearer in the county.
A few months before the pension,
his own immune system

went haywire and he died of pneumonia
and its complications.

Paul in his coffin, electric shears
beside immense fingers.
Beyond language now. His ex-wife
comforts the son who is a dancer
and the daughter so beautiful
she seems imagined
by Vermeer.

I walk the back fields in autumn,
noting the blight, the reduced yield of apples.
Trees go unpruned.
I think of Paul, this darker self
born of silence, moving among his sheep,
each grunt understood perfectly,
translated into hay, grain,
a hand pausing to rub
between the ears.

Sasha

Like any normal boy, Sasha plays
with puppies, laughing
at their antics, the surprise tongue
in the face, the quick nip on the shins
or pant-cuff. On his birthday,
he thanks his farm hosts
for the sunglasses and ninja turtle
teeshirt, which he rewraps
to take home, plastic containers and all.

So far, he's lucky.
He's not the boy with flippers instead of legs
in the photos by Victor Shuba,
or the newborn without arms or genitals
from the contaminated regions.
Five boys his age sit on the steps of an abandoned school
in the village of Bartalamejeu
eating radioactive apples.

Back home, he may treasure these gifts, relics
from his pilgrimage to clean air.
More likely, he will sell or trade them
for food outside the classroom
where the shattered globe lies on the floor
like the shell of a cracked egg.

Happy Valley

Among the well-groomed farms and restored cottages,
less than a mile from Pleasant Corners School,
where the walls are covered with paintings that show

a mother and child amidst flowers, a radiant sun,
spokes of light resembling the janitor's hair,
and a spiky dog who plays the stick family's best friend,

there's a businessman named Mr. Love who sells
his guns on late-night television, 1-800.
He has no time for children's art in Pleasant

Corners or in Guatemala: villages burning,
animals and kids wandering lost, stick soldiers, a myriad
of asterisks as explosive bursts, and a warplane

as a stand-in sun. The high-powered weapons he sells
are assembled in a reconditioned barn
by ordinary people, a lawyer and his handyman,

a secretary typing invoices, people you meet at the IGA
or music recital, who comment on the price of oranges,
all perfectly legal, like any other business—growing corn,

sugaring off—with the sanction of governments.
Death by direct mail, Bulgarian mausers, faxes to Prague
to exchange computers for assault rifles,

and the National Defence contact who visits
the establishment and stays for the barbecue, a few beers
on the patio, talks about his kids playing piano

and minor hockey in the capital, so keen on winter sports
they'd rather stay with granny in the Gatineaus
than accompany their parents to Salvador

or Guatemala City. Even that has advantages:
when the documents are signed, a few days spent
at the finca in Costa Rica, where the General's

daughters, mere infants when the operation started,
flirt with guests and discuss their professors at McGill,
one of them the contact's brother-in-law, security file

as long as his hair. Morality's a bore. Nothing
compares with the maples, hardwoods, and rolling hills
of Happy Valley. A perfect place to raise your kids.

Fusiles y frijoles

The choice is not simple for the squatting Indian
whose family has lost its land, whose
children have eaten only roots and grubs
in three weeks travel to the border,
and whose eldest son was conscripted
into the army a week before
the village was bombed. Light
from the burning church and storehouse
prevented escape and those villagers
not caught in the smoking rubble
were shot from helicopters
or forced to take refuge in a field of corn
subsequently torched. The sun rose
as usual to see the handiwork
of God's creatures, subversive trees
scorched into submission, difficult livestock
brought to their knees at last,
pacified, and Rigoberto's body, well,
I'm ashamed to repeat the disastrous litany
of what they extracted from him
and his proud, sweet daughter, except to say
her head tipped to one side like Christ's
as she hung in her torturers' strings.

If he knew the word 'hamlet,' the Indian
might wonder how it had been strategic,
too remote even for the guerrillas
who like electricity and tailor-mades.
Guns and beans. The lieutenant
holds the silk scarf of the Civilian Patrol

at arm's length. When the Indian
reaches for the white silk
that is so much more than a meal ticket,
the lieutenant gives him a pistol
and orders him to kill one of the enemy
to prove his loyalty. The word
he uses is *cojones.* A man,
bound and bleeding, is half-carried
half-dragged into the circle
by two soldiers
and dropped at his feet: Alfonso,
the schoolteacher from Parraxtut,
who laughed so much
and had carried the liberating words
with him from Huehuetenango.
His feet and arms are raw
and the thin wire cuts his wrists.
A blow, from a blunt instrument
or rifle butt, has closed one eye
into the grotesque caricature of a wink,
but he manages a bent smile
and says, above a whisper:
Do it, compañero, for the sake
of the niños. There will be time
later to mourn.

Yes, the children. The two who survive, wearing
Grateful Dead teeshirts that come down
below their knees, make strange
when he calls to them now
in the camp at Chiapas; and the beans,
joyless but plentiful, are sour
and metallic in his mouth.

Ice-Fishing at Vaudreuil

Days when perch and pike don't bite,
he's content to walk on water.

He moves from hole
to drilled hole,
inspecting each simple mechanism.
A small plastic flag
catches wind
and triggers movement in the line.

The older children race over the ice
on a skidoo,
while the youngest balances
on skates in a small circle
cleared of snow.

His wife emerges from the ice-house
and turns up the volume
on the car radio; a raspy
voice, wrapping itself
around the 12-string
twang, recalls the loneliness
of long-haul truckers
travelling through the night
in Oklahoma.

The Bees

All winter, as he motors through Africa,
Norman's bees, tributes paid, grow lean
in their chambered labyrinth of wax,
then hunker down to wait.

He'd worried whether to sell the house,
the hassle of uncut grass, water turned off,
kitchen heated slightly against the frost,
someone to store the car, prepare the hives.

One by one larks dropped from the sky.
Fields fell into a brown study; then
they were blank as foolscap, power lines
crossing the municipal road at an acute angle.

Near Khartoum, the jeep overheated
and his companions grumpy even in the shade,
Norman recalls, on the Ninth Concession,
a white charolais pasturing with a black angus.

Abandon your operatic style, counsels
the parasite lodged in his heart muscle;
move beyond the doctrine of use; be a thing,
bend close to the decaying earth.

He photographs dhows plying the brackish waters
of the Nile, elegant gridwork of Arab doors,
his mind restless in transit as it was back home—
in Canada, England, wherever.

Cancer took her; design jobs got scarce,
more technical, the aviation industry in flight,
computers, age; it might have been predictable,
but there were distractions, repairs to do.

The car starts, the cabin breathes a sigh,
the fields are green with envy. But Norman's
isolation remains, even as he watches images
of Africa take shape in the developing fluid.

Scouts, surveillance, long safari done, his bees
maintain the royal prerogative, prepare to swarm;
and Norman, hearing the hum of a hundred thousand
wings, bottles his chemicals and switches off the set.

In the garden, he witnesses the burning bush,
the courtly deménagement, and his left arm aches
as if someone, taking his blood pressure,
has forgotten to remove the velcro tourniquet.

Bog Fire

Acrid smoke from the bog fire
adds its weight to dense fog
as the Steinberg semi
hurtles towards the slow-
moving vehicle
leaving the weigh-scales.

You inch past the inferno in your car,
yellow flares, the grim faces
of police and bystanders.
This time the dead are not laid out
under blankets by the roadside
but casually going up in flames from the security
of seat-belts, halfway through a talk-show
or Mozart sonata, morning coffee
still on their breath, the announcer's
voice growing faint in the static of burning fat.

Back home a blue heron
lifts from the pond
in ruinous
silence.

III. Two Moose on the Hunker Creek Road

The Sporting Life

What kind of training
enables a man to kill a woman
with a high calibre rifle
and head into the hills, moving easily
across packed snow, leaving little scent
and no tracks?

Snowmobile in driveway, ridge
of low hills overlooking Crag Lake, two
stainless steel chimneys, a double swing-seat
hanging in the porch, and across the photo
a broad plastic band bearing the warning:
"Police Line Do Not Cross." In French:
"Passage Interdit."

An independent woman is a threat
to the abuser, whose wife stays home
out of fear. Big game guide
and taxidermist, he prefers his women
docile, stuffed, and easily mounted.
This stranger to the area, an engineer
for the City of Whitehorse, a land claims
negotiator who lived alone and was
capable of bucking wood, building
an addition to the cabin
at kilometre ten on Tagish Road
without the help of men,
crossed the line

into forbidden territory,
intervened. For this,
she encountered a claim that could not
be negotiated, blasted a hole
in all her arguments.

Reporters for the *Yukon News*
and *The Whitehorse Star*
adhere to the protocols of investigative journalism,
using only the word *suspect,*
though one speculates on the danger to people
working with battered women
from men who have nothing to lose.

Mother and two sons in protective custody,
community in shock, and
and the killer at large with his anger, blond
mustache, list of names, and
possibly blue eyes.

Meanwhile, the emergency response team,
the pilot, and the police dog
and handler have begun the hunt,
men trained in the use of weapons, survival
in subarctic temperatures, who know
penetration precedes the sound
of gunfire. Layers of skin,
futile as plastic barriers.

Prospecting

As if nothing happens in a poem
except recall, words on a page
playing at knowledge.

I required an image and it was given
in the gaunt face of a mother
returning from the cancer clinic
in Vancouver, her
mouth sensual, her eyes
radiant in the dim, enclosed space
of the cabin

or stitches in the boy's jaw
stretched by a smile
as he tells me how his sudden movement
spooked the sleeping malamute.

Did any of this happen, the gold rush
a state of mind, authenticity
insufficient grounds
to stake a claim. . .

The plane banks suddenly
as if scribing an arc on the mountainside
and lands blind, sweeping to a stop
on the thin strip of ice
beside the highway.

It's not a question of new material, nuggets
washed down by freak storms,

sudden upheavals (surfaces
that don't pan out), but what is already
there, percolating, subterranean,
bed rock.
                Sitting as a child
in the foyer of the same clinic (Vancouver,
1947), my feet and bare legs
scribing a smaller arc between the metal chair
and magazine rack,
while cobalt tracks the tumour
in my mother's
womb.

Bonanza

Each year when the river floods, buildings
settle deeper in the earth, foundations
crumble, balconies yaw into the street.
Brothels, churches, saloons, it makes no difference

to the shifting ground. Not even the sun
cares to explain to the Chamber of Commerce
what's in store for the faithful, choosing instead
to winter in Florida and Waikiki.

Hoses washing gold from mountainsides
turn up the bones of mastodons.
Hey, boys, over here by the glacial pond,
plant-life for the asking!

No murder or mayhem, just boom and bust.
Bitter farewells echo the dirt streets, scarred valleys;
great throats sluice the last green shoots
that clutch the submerged banks of the waterway.

At the Downtown Hotel

Allen's an asshole. I knew that all along,
but still I stuck it out. Stupid, eh?
That's Alice. I can feel the spit
from the word *stupid* strike my cheek
as she reaches for a second beer.

The three women seated with me
are genuine sourdoughs: a nurse,
a civil servant, and ardent Alice,
threatening to become gainfully employed
now she's dumped Allen.

We're the only patrons. The others
are sweating it out with an amateur band
waging war on silence at the Eldorado.

I tell them Peter's story about recommending
further education to a youth who quit school
to work as a miner. The kid
pointed to Peter's dilapidated pickup and said:
Why, for that? I worked two summers
and I've already got a brand new GMC.

A rumour is going the rounds that a company
will put down a hardrock mine nearby
and bring in five hundred families,
but not to Dawson itself. Peter offered it
as fact, but Buffalo, who manages the airstrip
and only taxi in town, sounded skeptical.

I'm trying to figure out what keeps the town alive,
other than tourism and National Historic Sites,
but Alice hasn't finished with Allen yet, though
she's demolished both beers. The three women
are nodding and laughing. Then Pat says:
Ya, he was an asshole even ten years ago
when he was married to me.

Doing the Klondike Crawl

She remembers little of her father, who left the family
when she was only a child, but recalls him
coming home, years later, to remove his books
and how his estranged wife clung to him, weeping.

Now she lives in relative isolation in the Yukon,
self-conscious about an unfinished degree
and wondering if her friend in Vancouver is right
when she characterizes northerners as misfits.

Yet she has owned two houses, building the second
when the first burned down, tried marriage to one man
and lived briefly with several others. She works
in the survey office weighing, above all, her options.

The mother who wept told her she'd have to make do
with other virtues, since she lacked the kind of beauty
that would attract men. A traveller listening at the table
is not untouched by the story, the strong face.

He wishes he could offer himself to prove them wrong,
but morning will see him gone, too, like the others.
He ponders, instead, the withholding mother
and the absconding father with his freight of books.

Sheet Metal

Tonight I'm a guest of Yukon College
in Dawson, its offices appropriately located
above the liquor store. Nothing like
a good foundation for learning, or knowledge
fortified. I look at the audience of fourteen,
all women, and remember
the metalwork manual given to me
by someone at the Whitehorse campus
to deliver here, the erotic terminology
stirring my loins. I'm not sure
about *the scratching method, flame hardening,*
or *single fillets,* but I think I understand *lap joints,*
cooling curves, and *sweat soldering.*
Did Elizabeth Barrett Browning count
these ways? Could Scheherezade have held out
another thousand and one nights if she'd owned
an acetylene torch and a copy
of this manual? I'd better shape up
and start reading some poems;
they're looking at me
as if I'm the Tin Man and not wearing a shred
of clothing. All I see on the page
in front of me are the last three definitions:
quenching, tempering,
and *better stress distribution.*
Have to face it, I'm
getting rusty.

Where Is the Man From Glad When You Need Him?

We stop to deliver Peter's garbage
at the community dump, beside the ski hill
and cemetery, with its separate sections for Catholics,
pioneers, and dead mounties. Most of the bags

are torn open and scattered in the box
of the pickup, whatever has not been spread
by ravens over the parking-lot at the local
TV station, where we're due to appear

in the afternoon. Peter doubles as Director
of Recreation for the City of Dawson
and local impresario and has bribed me
with sight-seeing in exchange for an interview

which no one will see unless they've had the channel
on display for its Noticeboard and taped music.
He tells me he's seen two ravens fly off
with a bag of garbage between them, shameless

undiscriminating scrounges, creatures a poet
might identify with. Later, when the camera starts to roll,
catching me off-guard pulling a face, stuff
goes out into the insulated homes and staticky air

that even the ravens won't touch. Sarcasm,
sick jokes, we're on a roll. Maybe I'll be the latest
casualty, another southerner who came to visit
and stayed twenty years. The director of wrecks,

playing host and cameraman, slips out of the frame
long enough to zoom in on his guest reading a poem,
but I'm too busy playing to a captive non-audience
to notice. Panic, where the hell has Peter gone?

I see my image on the monitor frantically
scanning the parking-lot, where two ominous
black vans have rolled to a stop. The phone lines
are lighting up. I hear myself talk rubbish:

art, skiing, cemeteries, it's downhill all the way.
How can you not love a place that provides
segregated gardens for the afterlife, that gives
its dead and garbage such a view?

Two Moose on the Hunker Creek Road

Peter and I bounce along the river valley
in his antiquated pick-up, windows cracked
from highway gravel and extreme cold.
He gives me a guided tour of the diggings:

names, statistics, dredges that lurched
like prehistoric beasts through the creekbeds,
disgorging dragontails of rock, creating
their own pools for sluicing gold, a No Man's Land

of lost dreams. Not that different from scenes
in *RoboCop* on the hotel television,
a high-tech shoot-out that leaves a hundred
dead and none of the moral issues

addressed. Chicago and Dawson City (a misnomer,
really, its population down from 30,000 during the rush
to 1854, not counting the full-term pregnancy
sharing my flight out), testimonies

to ambition and greed, sister cities
to Coventry, Hamburg, Nagasaki, Bagdhad,
and Sarajevo, places to try out the new toys
and the new vocabulary—*smart bombs,*

collateral damage, ethnic cleansing,
progress. Conscience itself, obsolete and expendable
as tonsils or baby toes. Peter is looking
for a spot to turn the truck around

when I spot two moose on the Hunker Creek Road.
The awkward grace of their large hooves
so carefully lowered into the waste-high snow,
the ridiculous elegance of those tender

foraging mouths, and the vestigial hump, bearing
the burden of past knowledge,
implacable disaster inching like a glacier
toward the silent, pasturing herd.

IV. Relative Humidity

Coming Up For Air

When light recedes and water closes over the metal
casing, you don't panic; your hands inspect
connections on air-hoses, brass clamps
tight around the helmet base
and little windows.

You inhale deeply to regulate your breathing
and hear, down the length of air-hose,
the reassuring heart-beat
of the pump.

Cells
smile in their dependency;
blood-race dwindles
to a trot.

¤ ¤ ¤

You meet in the lunchroom at Kelly Douglas
in November, foghorns
in the harbour, Lions visible
above the cloud-line.

Later, when you kiss her hair
in the elevator,
it smells of tea leaves.

Darling, you whisper.

No, she replies,
darjeeling.

¤ ¤ ¤

Something about elevators.

No time to decompress, the boss
stepping into the lift
as you stuff the contraband cookie
into your mouth. So
surprised, you offer him one.

Shafted in the leanest of times:
from imported tea and biscuits
to the flower business
on Alma Street.

She's beside you in the front seat,
hair done up in a bandana.
Fresh manure in the box of the dump truck
wafting in the windows.

Quel bouquet, she says, crooking
a little finger and screwing
her mouth up,

Formosa oolong.

Laughing so hard
you stall in the middle of the intersection.

¤ ¤ ¤

You descend the ladder
at the side of the diving-tender, the water
40 degrees Fahrenheit.

A hundred yards offshore,
light rain, a gauze mist gentling the cedars.
Crew in slickers.
You notice Johnson's turtleneck
frayed at the collar
from the action of his red beard.

Rain eases entry: border-blur, no longer two elements.
Kelp trailers, a half dozen coho
fighting the current.

Descent in stages, diagonal, even
with lead shoes. Grips
and cutting torch on your belt. Tin-pot
freighter, not worth the cost
in peacetime.

¤ ¤ ¤

Working alongside your own father
at North Van shipyards.
Crusaders in welding masks
move in their galaxy
of sparks.

Shift-bell. The foreman shouts
from the control shed—*A boy!*—and the yards
ring with the sound of hammers
on the empty hull.

So I invade the narrative,
slipping down the ways at Grace Hospital,
nine months pickled,
tidal,
amniotic, to store
in my mind your square mask
tipped back, torch in hand, grin
and slicked black hair.

¤ ¤ ¤

Insecurity, panache. The word *alma,*
Spanish for soul. Quadra and Bodega
at anchor nearby, a continent
hanging in the balance.

Saturday afternoon in Kitsilano, the trunk
of the blue coupé open and you
dispensing chocolate to a hundred kids
from damaged shipments off the waterfront.

Chocolate moustaches, the curb awash
with wrappers. Pied-pipering from blocks around
while she of the laughter and darjeeling hair
hangs back, embarrassed,
behind the screen door.

What eludes us lies nearest the heart.
Before Jules Verne there were no words
for what happens under the sea.

¤ ¤ ¤

Mixed signals, your body turned on from pressure
at sixty feet below.

Supply vessel, all hands
lost in fog. A tooth of rock
in the Narrows,
long gash
in the starboard bows. You imagine
the hole opening straight into the forward mess,
waterlogged faces startled to see this
arc of fire burning
in water.

Trying to work, force
of water driving you back against the hull.
Half hour's grace at slack waters, then the reversed
flow catches the freighter,
tilts it on top of you.

¤ ¤ ¤

To own
our emptiness,

times when the normal fare
of words and touch
won't suffice. Not that you

fit inside each other perfectly
like Russian dolls.
One is always wanting
in, for warmth,
or out of the suffocating space.

Something must break the shell
of vanity before it is too late
and we vanish
for good.

¤ ¤ ¤

Only the helmet saves you,
that extra cranium
of steel.

Twelve hours trapped until the tide changes
and the ship lists to port.

Gums ruined from the bends. Bones
ache, cells cry out
for nicotine.

¤ ¤ ¤

Rope of air pulls tight
around my throat.

I drink it in (speaking
of benders), strain

every nerve or sail as is
my bent.

¤ ¤ ¤

Blue light from the heart monitor reflected in the chrome
tank of oxygen beside your bed. Whatever joins us:
impeded blood, calculated fictions.

You return from war with a new wife
and a duffel-bag large enough
to hold me, laughing, kicking off my cocoon
of canvas on the lawn at 33rd Avenue.

Full fathom five. The cargo shifts, the poem
an unstable vessel.

You hear the sirens singing
at the Marble Arch Hotel on Granville Street
where addicts and streetwalkers in the adjoining room
go down for a third time.

On the bedside table, tiny bubbles line the glass
that holds your teeth.

Afterbirth

for Irene (Turner) Geddes, 1913-1947

Absence: the way the lost tooth drives the curious tongue
and alters, utterly, the architecture of the mouth.

First, there was nothing; then these relics appeared
in brown wrapping paper, with string
and requisite postage—

a cameo pendant with antique scrolled filigree
and a woman's face carved in profile;

a serving-plate,
Royal Staffordshire porcelain,
Cairo pattern, riot
of hand-painted flowers
on thick blue stems,
central ring of geometric swirls
that resemble an Arab carpet;
and, not exactly random,
fifteen peacock eyes
ringed in gold
and blue

fragments of your life arriving in the mail
after forty years, not exactly
post-haste.

¤ ¤ ¤

Ragged paintings fallen from the door of the refrigerator,
flush of cheek bending to lace my shoe.

Even your best friend Ann, married to a fireman,
could do nothing when wind shifted
and the burn went deep. So disturbed
she didn't take me to the funeral.

I entered the water at English Bay
and wandered too far along the crowded beach.
A policeman brought me back
from Main and Hastings, bathing suit
still wet, face smeared with neapolitan ice-cream.

Things I can't discard—fire and water, the blight
of the seemingly extraneous.

¤ ¤ ¤

Ann, who claimed the plate was seldom bereft
of cookies, also included

> *two plastic cigarette-cases;*
> *one for the coffee table,*
> *transparent with yellow lid;*
> *the other, wine-dark and narrow,*
> *with sliding lid for a purse*
> *or pocket, each bearing*
> *the name, Renee, or Irene.*

I recall Jim Friesen, his cold Mennonite name,
who cut owls and deer from plastic, the thin blade
of his jig-saw carving a delicate ear, how he

populated the basement flat in Kerrisdale
with his transparent creatures, keeping death at bay
and taming the fierce sheet-metal hopper
of the furnace, an inverted pyramid
of sawdust

¤ ¤ ¤

I was eating ginger snaps and nursing a beer
the evening of the CBC documentary
on prenatal growth. Last
of the night owls. There on the screen,
composed in its grid of amniotic dots,
the human ear, like the wings of Mercury,
seemed to sprout from a heel and work its way
to thigh and head, gathering as it went
its water music, coral
symphonies.

Womb, the place of generation

Cells multiply, run to excess. Cobalt
turns the tumour
into ash.
Would it were so.
Garden verses, my song rooting
in walls of soft flesh.

¤ ¤ ¤

Family legend has you playing piano
and singing *September Song*
or swimming the distance

from Fisherman's Cove to Point Atkinson,
just off the starboard quarter
of the boat. Days spent at Eaton's
as a demonstrator—lipstick, white uniform, sundry
foodstuffs. Then the contest at Orpheum Theatre:

MISS WRIGLEY'S SPEARMINT GUM.

¤ ¤ ¤

Mother is a dairy cow,
her breasts are made of silk.
Her life is an emporium,
her death a crematorium;
I love the taste of ashes in my milk.

Non omnis moriar.

Disassembled (or is it dissembled?) pieces,
something for the Orphic sailor boy
to chew on.

¤ ¤ ¤

No Grecian urn or enamelled vase,
only (I apologize for having to record it),

a slender tea-canister
of cheap tin
and made in China.
Four of the eight panels
sport dragons.
A figure in purple robes

and Fu Manchu beard
reclines on a couch.
Served by women
or solicited to buy silk;
I can't tell which.
Runners of a small sled
perhaps intended to haul
a wine-jug,
intrude into the scene.
Next door, the wise man
holds up a rock or fortune cookie
for an admirer to see,
or a disciple.
Behind the red fence
what's left of a stylized landscape:
rocks and trees, scrolls
of cloud, pine cones
the shape of hair brushes.

Details worn away, convex lid that measures leaves
no one can read.

¤ ¤ ¤

I squeezed the last drop of colour from the beleaguered
tea-bag and set about opening the bundle from Ann,
which contained an eight-page letter. Hieroglyphs,
things learned underfoot or by osmosis
in the womb, potent
waters steaming with plankton.

Years ago, in the room on First Avenue,
the visiting poet held court on a blue futon,
listened to my mother-stories,

rubbed the bassett's belly with her stockinged foot
until it ejaculated on the rug,
then said: *You speak with affection*
to cover up your anger.

¤ ¤ ¤

Wine dark, how the discourse
betrays us. And *bereft*, the dynamic
of transference; my own emptiness
assigned to a cookie-plate.

You at fourteen, stretched out full length
on the Star's running-board, or
younger still, photographed on the lawn
with different animals, your ringlets
perfectly framing the head
of the bulldog. So much of Vancouver
still bush, couch grass. Propped on an elbow
in the sand, pleated skirt
the scallop on the Shell Oil sign.

The migrating ear
never sleeps.

¤ ¤ ¤

Drop the spoon, the mother disappears;
undo each lace, she ties it up again.

The Chinese have a phrase, *yü-shih*, which translates,
roughly, as left-over history. If it's not
available, invent it.

Hours spent with Ann, shared laughter, room
for the outrageous, what is natural but otherwise
designated crude. My small face at your breast
and the husband,
remote,
dreaming a freedom
of uniforms, regimentation, perhaps
death, and how to forgive him
that, ever.

¤ ¤ ¤

Blue-veined placenta, my garment-shroud, buried
beneath the rose-bush in Kerrisdale. Assume
again this mantle of fire; play-thing,
mother-child, Scheherezade,
rehearsing your unforgettable cameo
in a pocket.

When the nightmares stopped
and your sad, concerned face
disappeared from the second-floor
landing, I felt the song
rise in my throat,
deep, plaintive, voice
of the lost tribes
of Israel, waters of the Red Sea
drawing back to engulf
Pharoah's armies,
and the cry

of those perishing
in the black and white stage-sets
of MGM.

Cairo,
the pattern more than serves
its purpose. Things
of beauty, things of no
account. Against such odds,
locating the words,
the mother-

lode.

Headlong Flaming

Fetch the binoculars, Tom, and see your poem
fly across the waters of Howe Sound
in the 16-foot Sangstercraft
we called The Drool, firing
at killer whales. You said
they drove away the salmon, ruined
business at the rentals.

I never questioned the logic
then, but recall with shame
my own adrenalin surge,
blood, danger, high speed chase,
light chop hammering the clinkered hull
off Passage Island, pumping
action of the 30-30.

Empty shell-casings splash in the bilge
or bounce off gunwales
into the chuck.

¤ ¤ ¤

His Majesty's Government regrets to inform you
that Flying Officer Turner has been reported
missing in action. Every effort. . . .

I was too young to decipher the telegram
but the eyes told what I needed
to know. An aura surrounded your return.
I worked overtime earning approval,
your stern face an enigma.

But it cracked open after hours
or when Morris, fresh from his dental lab
in West Van, nicknamed me The Rope
for hours spent jockeying boats
and disembarking customers.

A smile you might associate
with Lazarus.

¤ ¤ ¤

Kerrisdale's finest, wings clipped
for buzzing cattle during training
in Alberta. Commissioned in the RAF
as bomb aimer, the 'kid'
in the squadron, finger
on destruction. A full load
over Hamburg, a job to do
with minimal losses, the city
melted into timelessness,
bone china. Years later,
the nightmares, flak shifting
in the flesh of your back
and shoulder.

Milton's angels tasting fire,
condemned to walk among men, foreheads black
from carrying sacks of coal all winter
in residential Vancouver,
workers' caps and leather aprons
standard issue.

¤ ¤ ¤

Log Book:
March 7, 1945.
Time: 19:57.
Elevation, 11,900 feet.
John, the mid-upper gunner, is hit
and screams into the intercom:
"We've got company."
There's a Ju 88 on the starboard side, using
his navigation lights to distract us
from the Me 110 coming in on the port.
Below us Hamburg's
burning like a Christmas tree.

This my apprenticeship, rite
of passage, the text I must rehearse
again and again. Pilot
to navigator, pilot to navigator,
there's one closing in
at five o'clock, guns
blazing, zipping the flight jacket
to hold in John's guts, Vic baling out
without a chute,
Mel riding the goddam Lanc
to the end, sixteen
thousand-pounders and half
a tank of fuel.

¤ ¤ ¤

At the dock on Galiano Island
you slipped and went under,
no one nearby to haul you out.
I never asked if your training clicked in
and you folded your trouser bottoms

inside socks to keep out the water
and preserve body heat.
Survival routines,
all those times you'd prepared yourself
for ditching in the Channel.

You thought you'd bought it, so much
passing before your eyes,
enough surplus film to make six movies,
yourself turning end over end
until the chute opened
and you were jerked upright
above the inferno.
My name is Thomas Turner,
number J36305,
my name is . . .

Later, on the forced march,
you and Howie would kill a soldier
in the forest, then realize
it was too dangerous to escape,
surprise on his face
as his punctured lung
filled with blood.

Liberation, when a pack of cigarettes
would buy a pig. You watch from the sidelines
as the transport of POWs,
guys you'd eaten with, shared stories,
crashes on take-off.
Deafening noise and hands dragging you
like dead meat onto the dock.
Don't tell Doreen, you said, fear
still surfacing in your eyes.

¤ ¤ ¤

Two blackfish surface
near the rocks at Jordan River,
light reflecting off their flukes
and dorsal fins. Survival
a fluke too, twenty-seven missions
with odds of ten percent.

No safe hiding, oxygen
depleted, a soup of chemicals
that destroys sonar, renders perilous
for whales, for all of us,
the sheltering depths.

¤ ¤ ¤

Fall in, T-T, my madcap uncle
—in line, that is.

Forget the bald eagle, stuffed
and mounted over the television, no
forgiveness in its fierce eye,
no mercy. You, whom I love
above all others of that time,
must join me now, tour
of duty not over, the migratory
passage to perdition
incomplete. We'll gather the injured
in our arms, the dead
who have hung around waiting
for a gesture, a kind word;
we'll fly in the face
of instinct, tradition, whatever
refuses healing, defuse the unexploded shells

corroding quietly in farmer's fields
and at the bottom
of the sea, our only ark
a covenant of hope,

the rental agent
holding in his hands
a length of rope.

Home Movie for Unemployed Nymph and Satyr

This is the flick I never made, with jump-cuts,
and embarassing close-ups. Those feckless,
blood-riled days we ransacked
the moss-bed above the rocks at Tunstall Bay,
equipment hand-held, everything out of focus.

Awk! Awk! the gulls scream,
swooping out of the sky to investigate,
seeing only pale flesh, full of itself,
spit of seed the wind flings back,
flat underbelly of mudshark
in the shallows, its own fluorescent liver
the price of tasting fire.

Sunlight reflected
on centuries of crushed shells.

¤ ¤ ¤

Beachcombing the Vancouver years:
chips and triple-o burgers
at the White Spot, little mountains
of desire, lions looking on undisturbed,
their paws neatly folded.

Lights flick on in the suburbs of the heart,
flesh yodels above the fog-bank, dogma
strains at its leash. Afternoon

shifts, case-room, interns,
nocturnes, emergency, Mr. Abernathy
closing his eyes so the taste would intensify—
the dying, he said, can't afford to waste sensation
—special deliveries, ice-cream, cantaloupe,
happiness in 'General,' 1800 miles without sleep,
parking on slopes because the starter-motor failed,

a painted ship that sailed into our lives
at Lost Lagoon and made us
anchorites, contemptuous of riches.

¤ ¤ ¤

Or remembering Eric dead at his typewriter,
an uncancelled IOU linking him to us.

Afternoons in his Anglia rattling through Berkshire,
sucking marrow out of chicken bones
on Wokingham Road, gravestones
instead of mountains, traffic
washing the redbrick, Eric
the Red, providing cash
to stake a last Atlantic crossing
for two penniless colonials.

I believe he loved you
and must, at times, have thought me mad
to give those married hours to books;
yet he was a solitary man, his Aussie blood
schooled in distance, and he found
ideas so companionable

he lost track of time, forgot his medications,
and the constricted bronchial tubes
went into spasm.

¤ ¤ ¤

History, its layers,
cataclysms.

Foreign objects, alien
technology. The word *diaphragm*,
stretched over the cervix, dilated membranes.
Afraid of the body's graffiti,
imperatives.

Harrison Hotsprings. A honeymoon
without reservations? Why not,
someone else was enjoying
our pre-booked room.

The grinning bellhops placed a king-sized mattress,
on two single beds. One adjusted
the metal frames to reduce the shortfall;
the other leaned his weight along straightened
arms to test the springs.

Hot, indeed. An altar of sacrifice,
my inexperienced knees more bruised
than those of a penitent.

What I needed, even more than technique,
was words, laughter, and another bottle
of Harvey's Shooting Sherry.

¤ ¤ ¤

Drunk but not on honeydew:
information junkie with a million books
at my disposal.

Ashamed of my own ineptness at sex,
I played the virtuoso, voluptuary,
those stacks my boudoir and training-ground.

No spine untouched, no jacket unopened;
passions indexed, inhibitions tabled,
I learned chapter and verse, thought of you
periodically, held concourse
with fictional characters, plotting
a fine revenge.

I lied to keep from hurting you, said
it was over. My heart
disfigured like a cheap paperback
left open on the table.

I published and perished;
our child greeted me
with a smile, as if I were still visible
and had not betrayed
you both.

¤ ¤ ¤

All the energy expended in courtship
turned sour in the canned soup section of Safeway
in Powell River, arguing about prices
when what I wanted to say
was *Help me.*

News of your suffering
comes to me now. Another man
unable to talk of the body
though he builds limbs
and lectures at a university.

Pride. Long before the arteries
clog, the heart itself
hardens.

Your touch, delight
you took in learning, nursing
the same fires in me,
in Jenny.

For you I celebrate the foraging gulls,
oysters and clams who transform their private hells
into sustenance and beauty,
make love as best I know how
to schools of sleek salmon nosing the rocks
off Bowen Island, who gauge
from whence they come
and will return.

O, ye fishherds, how bright the scales
that stud your waistcoats!

The Juniper Lecture

The sermon, lame, awaits the healing touch
of silence. Airs sags with intent.
Eyes not old, but presbyopic,
fix on heaven.

A certain man had two sons:
the terrible specificity
of namelessness.

From under the black wing
of the piano, notes
lift off and congregate outside
in staffs of branches.

Trees, without protocol or preamble,
sway in judgement
over all that is not prodigal.
They dance, they dance,
these wild presbyters:
offering the whole shebang,
not some comfortable percentage.

They bend to where
all true believers bend,

to breaking.

¤ ¤ ¤

So he wasted his substance and inheritance
on riotous living,
thinking the claims of flesh
a sacred fire.

Hotel rooms,
lonely assignations.
She with the blind child
and silicone breasts;
those I might have comforted
with words.

To make an art of ignorance,
playing out that old movie
rooted in the cells.

¤ ¤ ¤

Your bedtime
in the house on Glen Manor.
You careen the length of corridor
to greet me, breath held
in the marvelous act
of balance and propulsion.

Juniper, my Juniper.

At twelve months
a bundle of small achievements
and bulgey pink sleepers.
We sniff each other
and make small noises,
satisfied, familiar.

A box of books under each arm
and heading for the Queen Street car,
I can't look at the woman
whose eyes and smile
you've copied.

¤ ¤ ¤

Sweet is the juniper
but sharp its boughs.

A certain fierceness, your soul
tempered in solitude.
Questions I could not answer
—there from the outset.

Age two, above the din
of Niagara Falls:
Mommy, what's the water
doing that for?

The curious gravity
in your face.

¤ ¤ ¤

In the plane from Guilin to Canton
I can hear you laughing with Wang Hongjie
about the values of contemporary Chinese culture:
the complimentary key-chain ornament with a dead fly
preserved in plastic. And how you used to think
Confucius another name for Anonymous.

Wang not knowing how to interpret
the feelings you inspire.

All of us translated bodily from earth
to heaven in a recycled DC 8,
racing a Force 7 hurricane
twenty-thousand feet above the Celestial Kingdom,
water dripping from the fresh-air vents
and only your infectious laughter keeping us aloft.

¤ ¤ ¤

You sit beside me
in this place of worship,
your head bowed. Not in anger
but in prayer, asking nothing
but a little light.

The parable of talents,
the healing oils.

Forgive the absences,
unshared measles, shoe-laces, school
reports, popcorn, bird-houses,
allowances,
the macaroni dinners
I never made.

Forgive me
for not loving your mother enough
and for being only,
painfully,
mortal.

¤ ¤ ¤

Desert shade, dynasty
of failed command.

I rise to go.

This Christ of yours
is not a one-night stand;
your precious laugh's
my fatted calf.

Miscues & Miscalculations

for Sarce

There, on the corner, two doors down
from the rented house on Broadway,
your small shoulders shake with grief
for the indifferent kids across the street
in whose games you remain invisible.
We've slept late, leaving your breakfast

of cereal, raisins, and milk on the table,
too immersed in our dreams
and appropriations to take much notice
of this diminutive actor on the sidewalk,
crying, *Why won't anyone play with me?*
then taking my hand and leading me back

to the brick cottage with its blue trim, porch
and playhouse swarming with frogs.

¤ ¤ ¤

At three you looked up at me—blue eyes,
blue ice—where Brown's Inlet meets the canal
and said, with perfect logic: *I don't want*
to skate (I'd asked the reason) *because*

I don't know how. Self esteem.
You'd never compete in races at school
or play sports, not willing to be judged
and found wanting. Does blood

make a difference? I refused to believe
it did, adopted you, our matching
insecurities, afternoons in the children's seat
of the old Raleigh bike in Ottawa, making

capital of flowers, burgeoning trees, your
short blond hair luminous in the wind.

¤ ¤ ¤

Grandfather so keen to teach you to tell time
he never noticed the fear in your eyes
as he flashed his home-made cardboard
clock with its easily adjusted black hands
and you chalked each humiliation
like a whip-stroke on your small back.
Now, a little better informed, we'd call it
a learning disability; but then, gentle

as he was, exasperation flooded his voice
as numbers went unrecognized. Time,
that old cheat and abstraction,
invented to subdivide our lives into neat
units: work, play, sleep, meals, double-entry
bookkeeping, ledger of failures and losses.

¤ ¤ ¤

Most painful to record, your twelfth birthday
on Victoria Avenue in Montreal, kids
throwing pieces of Kentucky Fried Chicken
across the rec room in the basement,

then stepping off the porch onto the right
front fender of the station wagon,
bourgeois scenario perfect to the letter,
except for me, the father, losing my patience

and striking you across the face with a folded
newspaper. World report, book page,
classifieds. Reasons, of course, but no excuse:

new job, new city, a floundering marriage,
displaced anger (small print calls it *rage*) stamped,
for a moment, on your wet cheek. Bad news.

¤ ¤ ¤

At fifteen you ran away with Spike
and spent four days at a campsite near Guelph,
until the food ran out and an infected bladder
made you wish for home, hair dyed black

for camouflage. I haunted the clubs
and night spots on Yonge Street, until someone
took pity and promised to contact you.
I'll never go back to fucking pumpkin-land,
you vowed, even as distance grew
between Spike and the retreating blue car.

What it added up to was compromise—
you knew that, even without a calculator
—power, too, in an act of defiance, the white
make-up and frizzed hair a chrysallis.

¤ ¤ ¤

All the discrete moments. Racing the dog
to discarded gum on the sidewalk, or scaling
Jan's fantailed goldfish (she holed up in the closet
to cry in private, her sandalled feet visible
beneath the suspended garments). Visits
to the General Hospital each time your nervous
stomach acted up, so quick to recover
we found you organizing wheelchair races

in Emergency. Our not noticing your eyes
were weak until grade three. You came home
from school and said: *I never knew before*
what the teacher was writing on the blackboard.

Talent, a gift for shape and colour: then,
the self-portrait in pencil and the polka-dot horse.

¤ ¤ ¤

You know what you want: a place
to put your mark on, children,
miniature troops so tenderly managed
they don't notice time passing,
all normal and desirable, but difficult
to achieve when fog rolls in
and obscures the numbers, the hour
and minute hands, when the pain
in headlines exceeds what is reasonable
and ones you need aren't always near
at hand or have made themselves
invisible again, rehearsing their antics
on a stage that you must re-design with script
and set and schedules all your own.

Cod Royal

You take your place at the piano,
adjust the chair, and lean
into the music. Your thin wrists poised
above the keyboard are the stately
necks of swans. I loved best

your earliest performance—how you sang
when the first wave of oxygen
broke across your scalp, flooded the lung cavities,
and drowned you into cadence.

So engine's hum is the amniotic
tide and the ticking clock
a surrogate heart.

¤ ¤ ¤

Each syllable a breast to drain, each word
an island asking to explore.

Lumblums, you said, as the sirens grew faint
in the rain-soaked night. Of those,
you were well informed, camping out in an oxygen tent
at the Edmonton General when fevers wouldn't break
and tepid baths brought no relief.

After twelve months of faulty diagnoses that left us
slumped over the catalogued symptoms
in medical dictionaries,
your tonsils and adenoids floated into history

down the storms drains
of the North Saskatchewan.

You clung to me in the doorway of the operating room,
blood from the hemmhoraging stitches bright
at the corners of your mouth, and said:

It's alright, Dod,
don't cry.

¤ ¤ ¤

Though Ecclesiastes never mentioned it,
there is a time for vitamins,
the horrible D variety that backs up the drain
and makes your mouth the floor
of a gutting shed.

You place your lips around the rubbery pill
and the effort to swallow
makes your small body shudder.

¤ ¤ ¤

I never knew you'd broken your collarbone
until you said, climbing stairs with me
from the basement,
Take my good hand, Dad.

For years I'd sit at the foot of your bed late at night
and listen to you breathe, inhale the newness.
Then you were in school, and studying piano,

your chubby fingers nowhere near the keys
for *Traffic Cop, Swans on the River.*

¤ ¤ ¤

Each year I mark your new height
in pencil in the entrance
to the laundry room

or count feet
and syllables in the dream
that is summer, my heart
crying

adagio, adagio,

your legs pumping, hair
thrown back, a brush-stroke of light
against the green of lawn, of
maples, higher and higher,
the relentless swing
a pendulum or

metronome.

¤ ¤ ¤

On your feet again, bowing, face obscured
beneath a canopy of hair.

My heart goes out, gives back the words
you shaped when the hours were
long, the pill bitter.

You placed your red stool beside the kitchen table
and reached for the bottle of cod liver oil pills.

When I asked what you were doing,
you lifted the plastic lid of the garbage container
under the sink and said, with the authority
of a policeman,

no more cod royal.

¤ ¤ ¤

If, on the stage you inherit, encores
are still allowed, I leave this poem as record
of my request. Know, too, that somewhere

in the audience a drowned sailor, his swamped heart
rocking in its cage of bone, sings your praise
without intermission, his lungs emptied

of all utterance.

The Dream Bed

Driven by divers needs, whiff of extinction,
wind playing along fluted sandstone,
mushroom-shaped hoodoos.

My heart goes to bed hungry,
fossils of old loves clearly delineated
in its petrified workings,
limpid memories.

Here, at least, the medicine
is reported to be good.
Under their paint

the old ghosts
smile.

¤ ¤ ¤

A place beyond options,
language of bones.

Below me the river, the stream
unsalted, all that is left,

itself but a thin line
recalling ocean.

¤ ¤ ¤

I join the silent ones, gathered
on this mound to purge themselves,
ground only a great dying
could sanctify.

Words and clothes left in small heaps
at the bottom.

Hot coals, prick of cactus.
I can't recall the dialogues,
gothic in intent.

¤ ¤ ¤

Bone fever, not what you might think:
a stake in the future, one's
name in textbooks.

It doesn't pay the mortgage.

The rush, too. Frenzied youths
lighting out after dinner to sprint up slopes,
in case new rain exposed a femur.

So we dig, await the skeleton
that is fully articulated, that tells its own story
without invention.

¤ ¤ ¤

Remove, with care, the overburden.
Brush by hand; tidy up
with dental pick and toothbrush.

Spread glyptol lavishly over exposed parts.
Apply the plaster jacket
layer by layer.

A wise procedure;
we were never transported easily.

What do carbon-tests reveal?
After the great bang, dust covered the sun
and plants died. No other course to steer, alternate
diet, source of light.

Pieces of the puzzle still missing.
Horned creatures, awkward as always
with the blood's inheritance.

Sixty million years is not too long
to wait for wisdom.

¤ ¤ ¤

Even as river mud settled around my ankles
I could not resist the inevitable pun
on the word 'divorce.'
Deceit, betrayal, events no secular
shaman could dispel.

Flesh conspires its own survival and demise.
We ride the rapids of its descent
at our peril.

¤ ¤ ¤

Long after we perish red currant bushes
will explode with colour, weight
of fruit bowing them to earth.

White hair of cottonwoods, cicadas
in the branches hymning dawn.

We'll lie together absolved of grief,
our bones intermingled
among the roots.

V. Mao, Dreaming

Bethune, Where Are You?

Nothing to do but wait, the national
pastime. Books burning
rather than autumn leaves, scholars
again buried in red tape
or worse.

Bureaucracy spreads like straw-weed
choking new growth, flowers
by the hundreds.

Poets should administer death
to false reputation, bruises
to complacency; instead,
they sit on committees, administer
prizes, and regulate
the seasons by prescription.

Folly, you say, *folly*
as the amber liquid disappears
down your throat.

Always irreverent, stethoscope
dangling from the canvas
chair. I mourned, of course,
but blood-poisoning
saved me from a nasty
piece of work.

Is it true butterflies reject their mates
for larger cardboard replicas?

Smoke Screen

I liked you straight off,
baggy trousers, your face
with its slept-in look. A dignity
that did not need the support
of outside trimmings.

You seem a man
who would do his damndest
to die of unnatural causes,
I said, accepting the Gauloise
you offered.

Whatever men do is natural,
you replied. Disastrous, perhaps,
but still natural. Our task
is to reduce suffering
caused by such natural unpleasantness.

Unrehearsed, immune
to insult. You turned away
to urinate
while I was talking.

Staff all aflutter, smoke
snaking around your head
and hunched bare
shoulders.

How I Solved the Contradictions

Became an actor,
that's how, practised deception
on a grand scale, my face
a constantly changing mask:
restless eye, regulation
smile, my body on a swivel
playing to the crowd.

Who is surprised when I take to wife
a mediocre actress
and give myself to the staging of festivals
and enormous rallies?

I wanted once to be a poet, emptied
of all that is not myself—
language, custom, idea
—to learn the meaning of stasis,
existing only in forms I made,
suggesting motion, energy in repose.

I led armies, relocated
entire populations and left my face
in a million public places,
when all I wanted was words,
precious words,
rooted in the human heart.

What I've Noticed About Longevity

Xiao Duan
did not rise in splendour
from imperial ashes,

but the phoenix crown
she wore
did.

Be Careful Whom You Invite to the Party

Stalin held me in contempt
though his Slavic face was itself
a study in Orientalism.

Like stock brokers, we'd made our reputation
on futures, paper dragons.

Ersatz lives.

He fears his own propensity
for metaphysics,
you said.

I let you watch them place eleven needles
along my meridian.

You called them stations of the cross,
suggested a modest current
for greater stimulation of the nervous system.

I was not prepared for peace, its
complications. A siege
mentality—that much
The Bear and I had in common.

No character for diplomacy in our
respective scripts.

Self-Criticism

Troubled faces fill our dossiers,
humiliations multiply
among the double-digit entries
in large ledgers.

If they say I am a monster,
believe them;
if they call me a saint,
don't be too quick
to dismiss it.

A billion people eat
more or less regularly now, some of them
too much.

The five characters most commonly used
in Chinese literature
are as follows:

money
tribunal
solitary
night soil
departure

I find the same concentrations
in Sartre, Steinbeck,
and Dickens.

A Fine Revenge

Born December 26, on the heels
of good news. You would have called it the triumph
of random particles.

Shaoshan busy now capitalizing
on my fame; why not, I
never meant to keep them poor,
and who knows when the spell will lift?

Here's the 'Mao Family Restaurant,'
specializing in braised soy pork
and sweet potato chips, supposedly
my favourite dishes;
and there's the button factory
cranking out my face
and slogans.

The miniature plaster busts they sell
for profit are mass-produced and primitive,
but capture my bulk,
stolidity, and retreating hair.
Retreating reputation, too,
my image dwarfed and beggared
by the meanest sergeant
in Ch'in's potted retinue.

About the fabled gift of tractors
returned unused from Shaoshan to Shanghai,
I told them my hometown must rely
on its own initiative.

ABC of Politics

I'm not surprised to see Deng
turn against the students

shouting slogans in Tien An Men;
he remembers the ones

I sent with red armbands
to march him through the streets

of Beijing, spit from the jeering masses
oozing off the dunce-cap

and dripping from his forehead
into eyes and mouth,

and those who taught his son to fly
from the apartment window.

Education's still a sacred trust
in the Middle Kingdom.

Flowery Combat

Hong Kong throbs: an infected cunt
ringed with neon.
I'm beginning to sound
just like you.

They want it so bad
they can smell it,
those were your exact words,
talk so unrefined
we called it Canadian Crude.

I held up the example of Marco
and the Great Khan
to no avail. My captive westerner
didn't want to talk
ideology; more interested
in getting laid.
Practical, you said;
there's work to be done
and no use being distracted.

You loved our name for it
and went on about bees
fumbling among the layers
of petals.

You accused me
of wallowing in history;
only a man who's never experienced
quicksand could be so naive.

Sex, freedom. Nothing
travels fast in China, except rumour
and disease.

The Great Leap Forward

Of course Lin Bao was right.
I was ignorant
when it came to agriculture,
though my father
had been a landlord.

It takes a hundred years,
in the best conditions,
to produce one inch of topsoil.

My insistence on wheat
instead of livestock,
produced only
crop failure,
erosion, sand
covering the ancient grazing lands
of Kublai Khan.

A jazzed-up version
of the Communist polka:
one step forward, seven
centuries back.

Ding Ling

Twenty years of silence.

Now she's dead, the stories multiply.
Her own friends among the writers in Shanghai
accuse her of purchasing survival
with sexual favours, after the Kuomintang
had killed her lover.

Others assume her long sojourn
in the countryside resulted from the essay
she published shortly after Liberation,
attacking our leaders for dumping
uneducated wives in favour
of young city women.

It's all rubbish. I wanted her
from her first communiqué to the troops,
the fearless prose, the metaphors
that made our fantastic project
seem possible. She might have loved me
if I'd kept to the path, but she knew a taste for power
would fuel my war with words.

She never wavered in her faith in language.
Two decades under arrest,
with neither paper nor audience, and still
she claimed our failure one of style,
not substance.

What did you learn all those years
in the countryside, the foreign student asked?
I learned a lot about chickens,
she said.

Watchdog Night

No animals here. Why
would they track us down
in the afterlife? A second chance
could cost their shadows.

Still, I miss them, recall your chicken
imitation; my pig, your moose,
your loon, my wild goose.

Then you were on your feet,
a whinny so sad I felt the hair rise
on my neck, echo
reaching us across the lake.

To you, a stranger, I might have
confessed it all: the lies,
the forgeries, the defenceless
child, the undercoat
of shame.

Wu-tai cautioned about the noise
and cigarettes. Pack-horses
restless in the compound.
We watched the lightning, its fancy
clothes, retarded speech.

Nothing is harder, you said.
than to die, piecemeal, in the eyes
of those who once loved us.

The Little Red Book

We never asked for opium, German beer,
or General McArthur

Marx and Engels were not exactly
household names,
when we started to recruit
in Hunan; no best-sellers,
just maxims jotted on scraps
of paper and slipped into the pockets
of peasants at impromptu rallies.

Within a few years of Liberation,
Beijing was full of poets
and scholars
translating my maxims
into other languages.

I asked the Costa Rican
how he had learned Chinese
and he said: I didn't,
I was too lazy; and, besides,
the English translation was so good
I worked from that.

Small Talk

Debate rages among intellectuals
about the nature of narrative, whether texts
are dependable, the life expectancy
of recipes. Those commissioned to write
histories made up fictions; what else
could they do, given the shifting
waters of language.

Officials with their local documents
and commentaries feared what is alien,
aberrant phenomena. Po Chü-yi
wanted his songs recited by those in power
and sung in the streets by expensive
prostitutes.
                    I looked for the *hsien*,
gods or divine beings, thinking
they would understand my choice
of the vernacular, which wasn't classical
or elitist enough for my detractors.

Is there nothing redeeming
in wronged spirits, dutiful servants,
and self-sacrificing lovers,
just because I gave them uniforms
and ordinary names?

I spend days in the library,
consulting the *Analects* by Confucius
and the *Book of Filial Piety.*
The texts are often faulty,
but they seldom lie.

Monkey Business

It's true, there were more important things to do
than keep an eye on you. Our comrades
in Spain warned us what to expect.
There's nothing holier or more boring
than recent converts, especially
the puritanical left, bloated
with self-importance like the frogs
we inflated in Shaoshan by shoving bamboo
up their assholes.

I told them I needed medics,
not saints.

I received weekly reports on your procedures,
of course: the collapsible operating table
made from truck parts,
used also for late-night poker
and majong.

Interns and orderlies
singing 'Sweet Adeline'
in English while performing surgery,
ostensibly for morale,
but also helping drown out the cries
of those who surrendered limbs
without anaesthetic.

Hygiene: an unfamilar word
that saved thousands of our lives
but not your own. Vats

of lye and pork fat
congealing into bars of soap,
sterilized instruments
covered in gauze to keep off flies.

The transformations hardly begun
as we lowered you
into myth.

The Longest March

All the great monuments reek of urine,
no one can locate the Buddha.

What will the people do when they are powerless at last
and no face greets them in the mirror?

Artists make me sick with their fashionable despair,
taking pleasure in predictions of apocalypse.

Did the phoenix grace this terrace with its
ashen song, or the wild goose?

My wife is dead, my children ignore me, I have
no vested interest in this legend.

Carp

A stone in the mouth
takes your mind
off the heart's depositions.

Some called you lucky,
what the English poet said
about dying young, reputation
more or less intact.

Hibiscus blossoms afloat
in the Garden
of the Lonely Administrator.

My mother in the distance, receding, her face
already blank.

I accept your presence
moving unseen in the murky dark
of the blood pool.

T.B., what's that? I asked,
when you spoke of inventions.
Two beauties, you replied,
laughing and making a brassiere
of your hands.

The taste of home.

After a while, only our failures
outlast us.

Making Strange

I took her in the north end
of the quarry, pushing
the material of her undergarment
aside. She held me so tightly
with her legs
while I thrust deep inside,
her shoulders only
broke the surface
of the water
once.

The girl was a driver
in the new unit.
We had been introduced
only hours before.
We talked of nursery schools
and egg-plant.

What I remember now
is not the boldness
of this public encounter,
but the difference in temperature,
the amazing warmth
inside her.

Sun and water always make me
want to fuck.

You laughed when I said that.

Auto-eroticism, you said.
The sight and feel of your own body
exposed to light and air
turns you on. It has nothing to do
with women.

Goddess of Disillusionment

Chung-huan warned
against lustful indulgence.

I was no worse than Pao-yü
with his mistresses and serving-maids.
And the exquisite Liu Lao-lao,
so dangerous in her brocade
and feigned innocence,
who wandered, half-drunk,
among the costly objects
of Pao-yü's empty apartment,
stealing a moment's respite
on his unmade bed.

It's not *hui,* the discrete event,
I remember, but the image
of her small breasts' rise and fall
as she tasted Pao-yü's absence
with each breath.

The word *breath*
and my all-too-brief career
as a biological conduit.

I exist now in the interstices
of matter, minute
spaces, history
leftover in the cracks.

Everything is provisional,
inter-regnum, the gap
between the beetle's striæ.

Chimera or optical
illusion, a red
chamber or the story
of a stone?

Forbidden City

A small bird
has built its nest

in the mouth
of the stone dragon.

Books by Gary Geddes

Poetry:
Poems, 1971
Rivers Inlet, 1972
Snakeroot, 1973
Letter of the Master of Horse, 1973
War & other measures, 1976
The Acid Test, 1980
The Terracotta Army, 1984
Changes of State, 1986
Hong Kong, 1987
Selected Writings of Gary Geddes, translated into Chinese by Peng Jia-lin, 1988
No Easy Exit / Salida dificil, 1989
Light of Burning Towers, 1990
Fiction:
The Unsettling of the West, 1986
Non-Fiction:
Letters from Managua: Meditations on Politics and Art, 1990
Drama:
Les Maudits Anglais, 1984
Translation:
I Didn't Notice the Mountain Growing Dark, 1986, poems of Li Pai and Tu Fu, translated with the assistance of George Liang
Criticism:
Conrad's Later Novels, 1980
Anthologies:
20th-Century Poetry & Poetics, 1969, 1973, 1985
15 Canadian Poets Times 2, 1971, 1977, 1988
Skookum Wawa: Writings of the Canadian Northwest, 1975
Divided We Stand, 1977
The Inner Ear, 1983
Chinada: Memoirs of the Gang of Seven, 1983
Vancouver: Soul of A City, 1986
Compañeros: Writings About Latin America , 1990, co-edited with Hugh Hazelton